IT IS
WHAT IT IS
Until it isn't

Lisa V. Taitt-Stevenson

ACKNOWLEDGMENTS

To my daughter Andayé, who inspires me daily, you are the epitome of everything I wished to be when I was growing up. To my son Amare', who not only reminds me to laugh, but forces me to laugh even when I want to cry. To my daughter Nette, you make this family complete and have shown me that love truly doesn't have to have conditions. To my husband, Tony, all I will say is *"Till my last day…"*.

To my circle, thank you for allowing me to "life coach" each one of you. In the midst of it all, you gave me far more than I could have ever given you. I love you all to the moon and back.

.

IT IS
WHAT IT IS

Until it isn't

1

Consider what you believe; yesterday's truth could be tomorrow's demise.

2

We tend to get upset when people don't take the advice we offer; consider that every person that sits at your table didn't ask to be fed.

3

Before you decide to hold off on pursuing a dream, ask yourself are you "reminding" yourself of a reason or trying to "convince" yourself of an excuse?

4

You must listen to your body when it says it's time to slow down or take a break. Today, be all ears.

5

Sometimes you need to step away and take in the view. Just because you see it every day doesn't mean it's any less beautiful or breathtaking.

6

Before you ask…yes, it is possible.

Go for it!

7

Stop taking your baggage to people who aren't equipped to help you carry it or discard of it.

8

When times get hard don't run from the process, just like with labor you must push through the pain.

9

Remember today always has the potential to be better than yesterday.

10

In all things, be S.U.R.E. – Standing, Unwavering, Relentless, Exorbitant.

11

Being in "Oprah's" presence doesn't make you Oprah; you still have to put in the work.

12

Though the darkness will inevitably come, remember the beauty remains.

13

Drama will cost you but happiness is free; take as much of it as you want.

14

Never forget the rare glimpses of beauty that can be seen in the rear and side view mirrors.

15

Imagine a world where love is the only option.

16

Create a space that reminds you that life is (indeed) beautiful.

17

Ask yourself if what you have always done is what you should continue to do.

18

Consider that love is not contingent upon you "liking" someone all the time. Take the time to tell them that in spite of...you still love them.

19

In order to move to the next level, you must first move.

20

Consider that every day has the potential to be the day that everything just clicks.

21

When life gives you lemons, why limit yourself to just lemonade.

22

DNA – Duplication Not Allowed Never forget you are one of a kind.

23

They say it's a small world yet so many of us manage to keep getting lost.

~Andayé

24

Anyone can "see" your value but if you want others to acknowledge your value, then you must create your own platform.

25

When your past shows up in a text, voicemail or IM, do you smile or cringe? Better yet, consider, did you plant seeds of blessings or weeds that you dread finding its way back to you?

26

Forcing your truth onto someone else is like offering an opinion that wasn't asked for.

27

Consider, we are bits and pieces of people we meet along the way; some things are meant to be kept and some are meant to be released. The key is to know which things stay and which things go.

28

When you look at your circle, consider you are looking at a reflection of yourself.

29

Guess who decides if today is a good day...you!

30

Consider that your truth doesn't have to be their truth.

31

What if today is the day that all arrows point to YES! Would you be ready?

32

Time to get out of "try" mode and get into "do" mode.

33

Are you faced with challenges or excuses that you use to excuse yourself from being exceptional?

34

Is your honesty the kind that allows people to make a choice or is your honesty the kind that allows only you to choose?

35

Why not be the person that, despite their challenges, can and will step into their greatness.

36

We all get tired; however, are you tired from building their dream or your own?

37

Take a much-needed
moment to breathe
and focus on you.
When was the last time
you took a minute to
focus on you? Take the
time you deserve.

38

Does how you feel line up with what really happened? Consider, a breakup doesn't mean you're unlovable; and a denial doesn't mean you failed.

39

If it's the world's praises that keep you going, what will you do when they give their critiques?

40

Are you going to make a difference today or are you going to talk about the people that are making a difference today?

41

If you don't like who
you were yesterday,
choose to be different
today. You are who
you choose to be.

42

Consider, life's journeys are not conquered by giving up, they are conquered by forging ahead.

43

Acknowledging the beauty within them allows you to see the beauty within yourself.

44

Just because there is freedom of speech doesn't mean you should always speak freely. Consider your words.

45

Never underestimate the power of "We".

46

In order to reach your goal, you must first establish it.

47

Take a moment to
breathe in peace and
breath out chaos...ok
on to the next task.

48

Don't tell them your worth, show them your worth in how you treat yourself.

49

Don't let your desire for perfection keep you from moving forward.

50

And vs Or...you decide.

51

Are you living a life of "AND" or Are you living a life of "OR"? Who says you must choose - having this "OR" that; you can have both this "AND" that.

52

The question isn't "What are you looking at", the question is "What do you see."

53

Don't let fear make your decisions for you. Last I checked, fear never ran a company, crossed the finish line, and never looked past the storm.

54

You are different!!! Stop living your life copying someone else, they've already taken that spot. Embrace your uniqueness. You are the only you the world will ever know.

55

No raindrop lands in the wrong place. Consider, you are exactly where you should be at this very moment. The key is to find out why. Do you stay and be still? Will this place take you to the next level? Is this place even about you?

56

After the smoke clears, love is what will keep it all together; whether it's your dreams, your relationship or your sanity.

57

At times, life can be like riding a bike downhill, even though you know you have brakes, you don't always use them.

58

It is in the midst of the storm that you learn who is willing to hold your umbrella.

59

Consider that when you truly become comfortable with yourself, others take on some discomfort. End result...you do you.

60

You can either be the person that brings out the best in people, or the worst. You decide.

61

Consider that when you straddle the fence it doesn't do anything but cause a pain in you're a$$.

62

Just because you stop digging deeper doesn't mean you stopped digging.

63

If you're going through hell, just keep moving; you'll make it through.

64

You have the power to choose. Who do you choose to be? Will you decide, or will your circumstances decide for you?

65

Time to turn the page of yesterday and start a new one today.

66

When was the last time you chose to dance in the rain rather than worry about if you had an umbrella?

67

Consider leaving auto-pilot mode, hitting the manual button and intentionally living out today.

68

If you want to ensure you have a restful sleep tonight, ask yourself if you are at peace with all the decisions you've made today.

69

What are you doing right now to ensure that at least one of your intentions today is focused on you and your goals?

70

If it's your way then own it, because if you cease to own it, it becomes their way.

71

How do you live your life? Like checkers or chess?

72

Consider that all you do has a rippling effect. Are your actions considered a pebble in the ocean or a boulder in a lake?

73

Allow your past to serve as a guide not as a resting spot.

74

What did you do today to ensure that today is "The Day"?

75

Sometimes to reach the top you must look at the mountain in pieces rather than as a whole; one step at a time.

76

Busy ain't always productive and busy ain't always busy. It's time to stop wasting time and start making intentional moves toward your goals.

77

When you say you love someone, are you saying you love their patterns or their potential?

78

What are you doing today to feed into who you are going to be tomorrow?

79

When your goal is on "winning", your focus is on you; when your goal is "not losing", your focus is on everyone else. Now ask yourself what have you been focusing on?

80

Before you get caught up in the dreams you have when you slumber, focus on what you see when you are awake.

81

Holding onto knowledge does not deem one powerful; however, it is the application of knowledge that will show where true power rests.

82

Just because you walked out of something doesn't mean you aren't walking into something else. Consider that every exit is actually an entrance into another place. So, what are you walking into today?

83

Always sharpen your creative tools, without them all you have is four walls but with them, what you can build is endless.

84

In the midst of all the rain, a ray of sunshine will always find its way to your doorstep.

85

Without involvement,
there is no commitment.
How can you commit to
something while standing
on the sidelines? Get on
the court, get involved
and commit.

86

Either you're passing through your past, or you're living in it. Consider that while you are living in your past, your future is passing you by.

87

This moment right now is all that matters as you will never have this moment right now ever again. Are you making the most of it?

88

Are the steps you're taking today bringing you closer to where you want to be tomorrow? If not, work on changing the direction of your steps.

89

Is what you do on a day-to-day basis Who You Are? Are you living your passion? If not, then why? What are you waiting for?

90

Sometimes you need to go back to the beginning where hopes and dreams are realized over a simple bowl of cereal while reading the morning comics.

91

Even in the rain birds sing, so why don't we. Remember, even in the downpours of life there are blessings.

92

Before you climb the ladder of success, make sure it's leaning on the right wall.

93

Rather than consider if the cup is either "half empty" or "half full", why not take a moment to acknowledge and enjoy the fact that you even have a cup.

94

Growth can be uncomfortable when you continue to try to fit into something that can no longer accommodate you. As you grow so should your surroundings.

95

The truth about your truth is that no one can take it from you...So why give away your truth to take on someone else's lies?

96

What do you do when you know you should be doing so much more? You do it! No more excuses! Let's get it!

97

This is the beginning
to making your life
your happy place.

98

Stuck in a place of knowing what you want but not sure how to get it? Sometimes the answer is quite simple. If you want joy, give joy to others. If you want love, give love. If you want material affluence, help others become materially affluent. Let's get it!

99

Most of us think we don't have enough time to do what we want to do...The truth is we don't have enough time NOT to. Start now! Let's get it!

100

Whether it's your time or someone else's, don't waste it; it's one of the few things you can never get back.

101

You want to test your integrity? How loyal are you to those who are not present?

102

Between one decision and the next lies our greatest power, the freedom to choose. Choose wisely.

103

Inner peace is the new success. What type of success are you striving for?

104

Are you pushing yourself as far as you can? It's not about beating what you may feel is your competition; it's about becoming better than yourself. Pushing yourself beyond your limits means you can and will create opportunities to move yourself from this level to the next.

105

You will never know the outcome of anything unless you take a risk. What are you holding off on? What are you in control of but refused to move on? What thing are you blaming on everyone else but it's really you who refuses to move and take the risk. The time is now.

106

When is the last time you did something or tried something new? If only for today step outside of your box and live beyond the limits of what you know. You may be surprised by what you learn about yourself.

107

Getting to work early means being able to walk the halls and hear your own thoughts before having to hear everyone else's.

108

When you blame others, you give up the power to change. Time to look within and take your power back.

109

The single biggest problem in communication is the impression that it has occurred. How often do you have a conversation with someone who hasn't actually heard you? Do you pause to ensure your message was received and/or understood? Or do you walk away assuming all is good? Consider all sides of communication.

110

When you take the time to build your team is when you will begin to see your dream become a reality.

111

Attempting to move forward while staring at what's behind you will make for an uneventful and unproductive ride. Don't look back unless you are planning to go that way.

112

Just like the moon comes out from behind the clouds, you must also emerge and not allow your talents and gifts to be hidden. You do the world a great disservice when you don't allow the world to be inspired by your greatness.

113

When looking in the mirror, are you able to see past the facade and if so, do you know who is staring back at you? Most important, do you like who is staring back at you?

114

To completely forget about your past almost guarantees you will repeat it in the future. Use your past as a guide not so much that it hinders you but propels you into the future you want.

115

When you wake in the morning, wake with the intention to operate in love. Operating in love begins at home and it begins with you. What are you operating in?

116

Regardless of how you feel about it, the rain will come and do what it's supposed to do and fulfill its purpose. So why when it comes to you fulfilling your purpose do you allow how others feel about it to dictate whether you move intentionally in it or not? We all have a job to do.

117

There is no place like home especially when it's your safe haven. There was a time I used to dread coming home but not anymore. My home is truly where my heart is.

118

Life is an occasion and just as the sun rises to it every morning so should you. What are you doing to rise to the occasion of today?

119

In the midst of the hustle and the grind take time to disconnect and refuel. Find balance while intentionally being the best you.

120

"Eyes forward, chin up, shoulders back" is what my mom would always tell me. If we never look down we may miss the beauty that lies at our feet.

121

Get your head up out of the clouds is what I will NEVER say to my children; That's where dreams are made. Up there, there are no limitations, no boxes to be stuck in. So yes, keep your head in the clouds and dream big and wide.

122

In the midst of the other clouds there always seems to be one that stands alone. It's not always necessary to be with the crowd to serve your purpose and make an impact.

123

What are you doing different today that will allow you to have a different tomorrow?

124

In the midst of enjoying the journey, one can never forget about the beauty of the destination.

125

Are you moving in your purpose, driving towards your goals, being intentional in your steps? Tomorrow waits for no one.

126

Never discount the small victories in life.

127

Train for happiness and success. Whether we know it or not we train our minds to accept and desire foolishness. We train to accept lies, accept negativity and accept what one may call failure. We've trained ourselves to find comfort in discomfort. With that same effort, why not train for happiness. Train yourself to look for the joys in life. It is in that happiness that you will begin to see success.

128

Many of us are walking past opportunities while time is passing us by. Whether inside or outside, the hustle must go on.

129

Always make time to work on your dreams, most days are spent building or maintaining someone else's.

130

If you're like most people, you feed your physical self at least 3 meals per day but how often do you feed your spiritual self? Do you rely only on one "meal" a week on Sundays? Imagine what your walk would look like if you fed your spiritual self as often as you feed your physical self.

131

Open road = Endless possibilities.

132

Opportunities don't stop so why should you. If it's not writing, it's life coaching, if it's not prepping for a workshop, it's contributing to another's dream. Refuel in between the hustle.

133

We all need to be reminded of not only our value to ourselves but also our value to others.

134

Life is about balance; in the midst of the hustle, stands the family worth the hustle.

135

With a new day comes new opportunities. With that comes the joy of realizing not only will you be receiving opportunities but you also get to offer some.

136

Dream it, think it, work it and most definitely achieve it.

137

Let them sleep while you hustle. Opportunities know no timeline.

138

One should always wake daily with intention. Intentional in your words, intentional in your efforts and intentional in your thoughts.

139

9-5 comes with a required dress code; hustle mode does not.

140

Change your perspective...you don't have to hustle, you get to hustle.

141

Don't focus so long on a closed door that you miss the open one.

142

Are you working on building your empire? If not, what are you waiting for? Start now.

143

At the end of the day we all need a safe haven. Where's yours?

144

Work deliberately
toward your goals.

145

Change the root,
change the tree.

146

Never forget or underestimate the power of your words. You can speak life or death into any situation.

147

Don't let fear stop you, just do it afraid.

148

Living intentionally means doing that little "extra".

149

Now that you believe, it's time to start putting in the work.

150

It's never too late to start making smart choices.

151

Just because no one else is moving doesn't mean you should lose momentum. Keep moving forward!

152

As much as we acknowledge that the struggle is real, we must never forget so is the hustle.

153

If only for today, be intentional in all things. It's not for everyone to understand so don't lose sight of YOUR vision.

154

Time to slay!

155

The hustle doesn't stop just because it's the weekend.

156

Let us all strive to be Kings and Queens among Kings and Queens.

157

I am perfectly
imperfect.

158

It is what it is until it ain't.

159

Life has a way of showing you who you are.

160

There comes a period in everyone's life when you must purposely create space and time solely for you. Where every breath is deliberate.

161

As you breathe in, breathe in life; as you breathe out, release the stuff within you that no longer serves a purpose to the person you are now.

162

My breakthrough is a true reflection of my been through.

163

Pause long enough to catch your breath but not long enough to set yourself back.

164

All things can be considered temporary...and for some, even death.

165

Be courageous enough to take your own advice first before offering it.

166

Consider what you deem is your worth, then double it, we all seem to undervalue ourselves.

167

Talk becomes cheap when you lose the realization of the value of your words.

168

Forgiveness or permission....you choose.

169

Walk in your calling, it's the one lane where if you listen close enough, your opposition will let you know you are on course.

170

Don't wait until you are drowning to ask for help, we all know when we are taking on water.

171

Motivation is like air, it gives you what you need to make it through the day.

172

If you didn't quite hit the mark today, don't fret, tomorrow is another day to get that much closer to your goal.

173

Mornings represent: New attitudes, new goals, fresh starts, new opportunities, fresh perspectives, new ideas, and another supply of endless possibilities.

174

At the end of the day, rather than focusing on what wasn't accomplished, turn your attention toward what was achieved.

175

Sometimes you just need to take a moment to acknowledge your own beauty within.

176

In most things in life there is a waiting period. However, when it comes to making the world a better place, you don't have to wait one single minute. So, what are you waiting for?

177

Consider that when you judge someone, it doesn't define who they are, it defines who you are.

178

You never know what anyone needs at any given moment. Just because they look fine doesn't mean you still shouldn't ask how they're doing.

179

Consider everyone plays a role in someone's life...are you aware of the role you play? Are you a friend or foe? Covenant keeper or devil's advocate? A distraction or motivation?

180

Finding balance is not like a scale that weighs equally on both sides; it is ensuring that you make the most of the time YOU have for YOU so that if everything else comes tumbling down, YOU remain standing.

181

Don't try to force anyone to believe you, the key is to just allow them to hear you.

182

Life is not about limits, it's about finding balance within a limitless life.

183

Whatever you are doing right now...stop and take a moment. Are you making a difference? Are you making an impact? If so...proceed, if not...change direction.

184

The worst business idea is the one not presented.

185

Some of our greatest lessons are learned from our adversaries.

186

Loving in the sunshine is easy, learn how to love in the storm.

187

Life will often present us with a nicely wrapped "gift" of chaos, consider you have the choice to either take it or give yourself the gift of peace.

188

I can love you, flaws and all, but when your flaws force me to question the love I have for myself, I need to love you from afar.

189

If you're wondering if the mess someone is giving you to carry is yours, take a moment to check the tag and you will realize it's not even your size. Stop allowing yourself to get weighed down with stuff that doesn't belong to you.

190

When you are angry with your loved one, intentionally do something nice for them. If you can intentionally love through anger, you can love through anything.

191

Balance isn't about quantity
but about quality. What
one can do in a minute,
others can't do in a lifetime.
Find YOUR balance, that is
the key to YOUR happiness
and YOUR sanity.

192

Are you getting tripped up by something that has nothing to do with you and your goals? Stay focused.

193

Consider when feeling overwhelmed, we all need something to reach for. You can GO to a place of peace, CREATE a space of peace or BE that peace for yourself or someone else in need.

194

Don't dim the light within you by being envious of someone else's. Admiration and acknowledgement will fuel your light, jealousy and contempt will extinguish it.

195

Right now is the only chance you get to make the most of this very moment. Now consider that by the time you finish reading this, that moment has already passed.

196

Sometimes you need to realize how lucky you are that you didn't get what you asked for.

197

If you do unto others expecting them to do the same unto you...you may as well not do anything at all.

198

Just because you are
charged to plant a seed
doesn't mean you are
also assigned to water it.

199

Are you "The One"? The one people can trust, the one people can turn to, the one people dread upon approach? We all are that "One". The question is, which "One" are you?

200

Consider every moment has the potential to be an educating moment; Whether you are teaching or the one being taught. The key is to be humble enough to receive and enlightened enough to teach.

201

What part of yourself are you feeding right now? Does the part you're feeding ensure you reach your goal? More importantly, is what you're taking in full of what's needed to forge ahead or is it just empty Calories.

202

How often have you gotten angry at a response merely because it was the honesty you asked for but didn't really want to hear? Consider, you can either not ask the question, brace yourself for the answer or admit that deep down you already know the answer but are hoping that someone will tell you otherwise.

203

A gift may come from your hand, or even your words, but it must be motivated by your heart.

204

In order to truly find inner peace, you must rest in the fact that your storms weren't weathered in vain.

205

When life happens, allow yourself to feel what you need to feel, realizing this is and can be a moment in time that will strengthen you and not break you. This is a moment in time that will reveal what you are truly made of. A moment in time that will show you who you can become.

206

You are whatever you say you are. The world can and will see you as it chooses, however, it is how you see yourself that indicates where the definition of who you are truly begins.

207

Learn from life's mistakes. Don't dwell so long on the slip-ups that you end up living in the mistake, pause long enough to learn the lesson and then move on.

208

Don't equate tolerance for acceptance. Just because it's been "working for you" doesn't mean it's been working.

209

We don't listen to what we hear, we listen to what we want to hear.

210

Stop trying to dive into irregular stuff when you can't even handle the regular stuff.

211

Is worry your companion? Maybe it's time to breakup.

212

We tend to discount the various roles we have by proclaiming that "I'm just a...". You weren't "just" created to be "just a" anything. Own who you are and shout it out to the world boldly, proudly and unapologetically.

213

Sometimes you have to take a much needed moment to figure out if it's a what, a who or possibly a you that is standing in your way .

214

The root of your unhappiness is the misconception that your happiness comes from everyone else but you.

215

You will become unstuck when the desire for your future becomes greater than the pain of your past.

216

If you are on course to truly living in your purpose, consider that no matter where you are, no matter how difficult things might appear to be, you are always being moved towards magnificence.

217

The growth of today requires the shedding of yesterday.

218

Just doing the stuff that comes easy is not the stuff that makes you, it's the push through, the break through, the "ish" that defines who you are.

219

The releasing of yesterday's crutches will allow you to walk freely into today.

220

Once you align your power with being powerful is when you will reach levels you had only thought to dream of.

221

No more rolling stops. Many of us leave before we fully stop. Take a minute to breathe in the space that you are in. Get what you are supposed to, learn what is necessary or give the part of you that is needed at that time, then move on.

222

In the midst of reading up on love, life, and finances, have you made time to actually love, live and be prosperous?

ABOUT THE AUTHOR

Everyone has their inner battles, the ones that no one sees. I grew up in Bed Stuy, Brooklyn with a love for dance and music. They were my voice and helped me overcome insurmountable obstacles. From the age of four I learned to be a warrior, this inner child is my engine, and her resilience continues to push me to levels I didn't think possible ...
On 9-11 I was once again called upon to rely on this resilience when I narrowly escaped the imploding buildings, and I was left to bear the weight of survivor's guilt. I vowed to help others and I rallied to summon my inner warrior as a pledge and a torch bearer. These words are the distillation of the inner wisdom of my soul. From my table to yours with love. I do not write anything that does not inspire or empower. I invite you to connect with passion and not just with pitfalls, and above all celebrate your triumphs!

Instagram: Authentic_Author911
E-mail: lwi.ltaitt@gmail.com

www.ingramcontent.com/pod-product-compliance
Lightning Source LLC
Chambersburg PA
CBHW061430040426
42450CB00007B/974